THE PATHOLOGY OF PRIVILEGE

THE PATHOLOGY OF PRIVILEGE:
The Econonic Consequences of Government Favoritism

MATTHEW MITCHELL

MERCATUS CENTER
George Mason University

Arlington, Virginia

ABOUT THE MERCATUS CENTER

The Mercatus Center at George Mason University is the world's premier university source for market-oriented ideas—bridging the gap between academic ideas and real-world problems.

A university-based research center, Mercatus advances knowledge about how markets work to improve people's lives by training graduate students, conducting research, and applying economics to offer solutions to society's most pressing problems.

Our mission is to generate knowledge and understanding of the institutions that affect the freedom to prosper and to find sustainable solutions that overcome the barriers preventing individuals from living free, prosperous, and peaceful lives. Founded in 1980, the Mercatus Center is located on George Mason University's Arlington campus.

www.mercatus.org

CONTENTS

What is privilege?

Bailouts are only the tip of the iceberg.

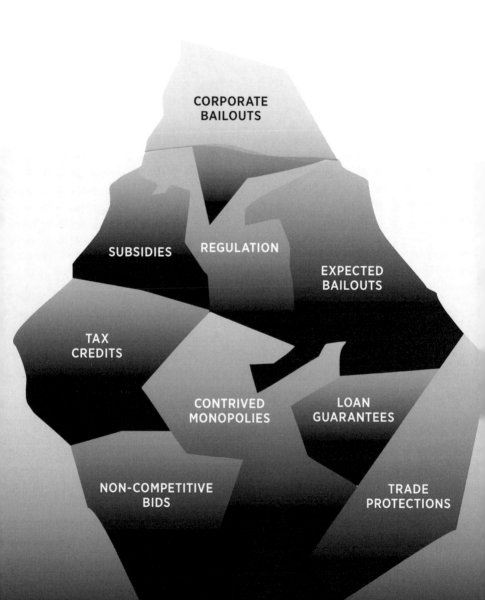

D espite the ideological miles that separate them, activists in the Tea Party and Occupy Wall Street movements agree on one thing: both condemn the recent bailouts of wealthy and well-connected banks. To the Tea Partiers, these bailouts were an unwarranted federal intrusion into the free market; to the Occupiers, they were a taxpayer-financed gift to the wealthy executives whose malfeasance brought on the financial crisis.[1] To both, the bailouts smacked of cronyism.

In this paper, I show that the financial bailouts of 2008 were but one example in a long list of privileges that governments occasionally bestow upon particular firms or particular industries. At various times and places, these privileges have included (among other things) monopoly status, favorable regulations, subsidies, bailouts, loan guarantees, targeted tax breaks, protection from foreign competition, and noncompetitive contracts. Whatever its guise, government-granted privilege is an extraordinarily destructive force. It misdirects resources, impedes genuine economic

---

1. According to Occupy Wall Street activists, "Corporations . . . run our governments . . . have taken bailouts from taxpayers with impunity, and continue to give Executives exorbitant bonuses." New York City General Assembly, "Declaration of the Occupation of New York City," http://www.nycga.net/resources/declaration/ (accessed April 30, 2012). And according to the Tea Party Patriots, "The Tea Party movement spontaneously formed in 2009 from the reaction of the American people to fiscally irresponsible actions of the federal government, misguided "stimulus" spending, bailouts, and takeovers of private industry." Tea Party Patriots, "About Tea Party Patriots," http://www.teapartypatriots.org/about/ (accessed April 30, 2012).

progress, breeds corruption, and undermines the legitimacy of both the government and the private sector.

I. THE GAINS FROM EXCHANGE

It is helpful in understanding any pathology to begin by examining the characteristics of a healthy state of affairs. With that in mind, consider a market in which no firms enjoy favoritism: all are equal in the eyes of the law.[2] In such a situation, free and voluntary trade results in gains for both sellers and buyers. Consider a simple trade: *A* offers *B* $6.00 in exchange for a sandwich. *A* must value the sandwich more than $6.00; otherwise he would not part with his money. Similarly, *B* must value the $6.00 more than the sandwich; otherwise *he* would not part with his sandwich. Though no new sandwiches and no new dollars have been created, the very act of exchange miraculously elevates the well-being of all concerned. (Figure 1 in the appendix, on page 39, describes the gains from trade using supply and demand curves.)

This simple idea—that voluntary exchange is mutually beneficial—is at the heart of modern economics.[3] Indeed, a national economy, with all its sophistication and complexity, is simply a very large number of mutually beneficial trades. And a recession is nothing more than a collapse in the number of such trades. Moreover, as individuals expand the number of people with whom they exchange, they are able to consume a wider diversity of products while becoming more specialized in production. Specialized production, in turn, permits greater productive efficiency and

---

2. In an interview with James Buchanan, F.A. Hayek once remarked, "[The First Amendment] ought to read, 'Congress shall make no law authorizing government to take any discriminatory measures of coercion.' I think that would make all the other rights unnecessary." Quoted in James Buchanan and Roger Congleton, *Politics by Principle, Not Interest: Toward Nondiscriminatory Democracy* (Indianapolis: Liberty Fund, [1998] 2003), vii.

3. This point is not disputed by economists. See, for example, the microeconomic textbooks by Paul Krugman (of the left) and Gregory Mankiw (of the right). Paul Krugman and Robin Wells, *Microeconomics*, 2nd ed. (New York: Worth Publishers, 2009); Gregory Mankiw, *Principles of Microeconomics*, 6th ed. (Mason, OH: South-Western, 2012).

allows us to do more with less. It is no exaggeration to say that the expansion of mutually beneficial exchange accounts for the lion's share of human progress.[4]

In a healthy market, there will be so much exchange that the gains from trade are maximized. This is more likely when markets are competitive.[5] And markets tend to be competitive when property rights are well-defined, the costs of transacting (negotiating the terms of trade) are minimal, and—most important—there are no barriers to entering or exiting the industry.[6] Markets can achieve competitive conditions with relatively few buyers and sellers. In a famous experiment, economic Nobel Laureate Vernon Smith showed that even when there are as few as four buyers and sellers, a market will tend toward the competitive equilibrium.[7]

II. TYPES OF PRIVILEGE

In the next section, I will review the various ways in which government-granted privileges diminish the gains from exchange, threaten economic growth, and undermine the legitimacy of government and the private sector. For now, consider the forms that privilege might take.

A. Monopoly Privilege

In April 2004, Chinese officials arrested Dai Guofang and sentenced him to five years in prison. Mr. Dai's crime was founding a low-cost steel firm that competed with a number of factories

---

4. See, for example, Matt Ridley, *The Rational Optimist: How Prosperity Evolves* (New York: Harper Collins, 2011).

5. There are exceptions. In some markets, up-front or fixed costs are so great that the competitive price is not high enough to make the venture worthwhile (think of a new drug, which can costs millions in R&D). In this case, the gains from trade are maximized when the industry is monopolized.

6. These characteristics appear in one form or another in most microeconomic textbooks.

7. Vernon Smith, "An Experimental Study of Competitive Market Behavior," *Journal of Political Economy* 30, no. 2 (1962): 111–137.

backed by the Chinese government.[8] The government, it seems, wanted to send a message: certain firms are privileged and it is illegal to compete with them. Monopoly privileges of this sort are more common in nations where governments direct large sectors of the economy.[9] But monopoly privileges are not an artifact of the developing world.

The United States Postal Service is a case in point. While the U.S. Constitution grants Congress "the power to establish post offices and post roads," it does not, like the Articles of Confederation before it, grant Congress the "sole and exclusive right" to provide these services. By the 1840s, a number of private firms had begun to challenge the postal service monopoly. Up and down the East Coast, these carriers offered faster service and safer delivery at lower cost.[10] While the competition forced the postal service to lower its rates, it also encouraged the postal service to harass its private competitors: within a few years, government legal challenges and fines had driven the private carriers out of business.[11] More than a century later, in 1971, the postal service was finally converted into a semi-independent agency called the United States Postal Service (USPS). Its monopoly privileges, however, remain. No other carriers are allowed to deliver nonurgent letters and no other carriers are allowed to use the inside of your mailbox.[12]

8. Daron Acemoglu and James Robinson, *Why Nations Fail: The Origins of Power, Prosperity, and Poverty* (New York: Random House, 2012), 437–438. See also Richard McGregor, *The Party: The Secret World of China's Communist Rulers* (New York: Harper Collins, 2010), 220–223.

9. See, for example, "The Rise of State Capitalism: The Emerging World's New Model," *The Economist*, January 21, 2012, http://www.economist.com/node/21543160.

10. Kelly B. Olds, "The Challenge to the U.S. Postal Monopoly, 1839–1851," *Cato Journal* 15, no. 1 (Spring/Summer 1995).

11. Ibid.

12. In addition to these perquisites, the USPS pays no taxes and is exempt from local zoning laws.

Privately owned firms, including local cable operators and many publicly regulated utilities, may enjoy legal monopoly protection as well.[13]

B. Regulatory Privilege

While it is relatively uncommon for U.S. firms to enjoy legal monopoly status, many firms do enjoy regulatory preferences that give them a measure of monopoly power. Until recently, for example, regulations governing banks, broker-dealers, and money market funds effectively required them to hold securities that had been rated by one of only a handful of private credit ratings agencies that had been blessed with a seal of approval from the Securities and Exchange Commission. This regulation may have resulted in more costly and less reliable credit ratings, but it was a boon to the three ratings agencies: Moody's, Fitch, and Standard and Poor's.[14]

Though business leaders and politicians often speak of regulations as "burdensome" or "crushing," the example shows that sometimes it can be a privilege to be regulated, especially if it hobbles one's competition. This insight prompted consumer advocates Mark Green and Ralph Nader to declare in 1973 that "the verdict is nearly unanimous that economic regulation over rates, entry, mergers, and technology has been anticompetitive and

---

13. Some of these firms have significant fixed costs, which suggests that the market might only support one or two firms in any event. This possibility does not imply, however, that there is an economic case for outlawing competition. See George Stigler, "Monopoly," in *The Concise Encyclopedia of Economics*, ed. David Henderson (Indianapolis: Liberty Fund, 2008).

14. The privilege grew out of a 1975 Securities and Exchange Commission rule that designated the big three agencies as "Nationally Recognized Statistical Ratings Organizations." Over the next 25 years, only four additional firms qualified for this designation. By the end of 2000, however, mergers had reduced the number to the original three. Lawrence J. White, "A Brief History of Credit Rating Agencies: How Financial Regulation Entrenched this Industry's Role in the Subprime Mortgage Debacle of 2007–2008," *Mercatus on Policy* 59 (Arlington, VA: Mercatus Center at George Mason University, 2009).

wasteful,"[15] and that "our unguided regulatory system undermines competition and entrenches monopoly at the public's expense."[16] It also prompted bipartisan support for deregulation or partial deregulation of airlines, trucking, telecommunications, and finance in the late 1970s and early 1980s.[17]

But in many industries, barriers to entry remain. Thirty-six states, for example, require government permission to open or expand a health care facility.[18] Thirty-nine require government permission to set up shop as a hair braider.[19] In the 1950s, less than 5 percent of the work force needed an occupational license; the number rose to 18 percent in the 1980s and it now stands at 29 percent.[20]

While barriers to entry impose costs on all firms, the costs are more burdensome to newer and smaller operators. This is why existing firms often favor regulations.[21] University of Chicago economist George Stigler won the Nobel Prize in economics for showing that regulatory agencies are routinely "captured" and used by the firms they are supposed to be regulating.[22]

In the nineteenth century, the Interstate Commerce Commission (ICC) was famously captured by the railroads it was

15. Mark Green and Ralph Nader, "Economic Regulation vs. Competition: Uncle Sam the Monopoly Man," *Yale Law Journal* 82, no. 5 (April 1973): 871–889, 881.

16. Ibid., 871.

17. On the benefits of this deregulation, see Clifford Winston, "Economic Deregulation: Days of Reckoning for Microeconomists," *Journal of Economic Literature* 31 (1993): 1263–1289.

18. National Conference of State Legislatures, "Certificate of Need: State Health Laws and Programs," http://www.ncsl.org/issues-research/health/con-certifi-cate-of-need-state-laws.aspx (accessed May 2012).

19. Valerie Bayham, *A Dream Deferred: Legal Barriers to African Hairbraiding Nationwide* (Arlington, VA: Institute for Justice, September 2006).

20. Morris Kleiner and Alan Krueger, "The Prevalence and Effects of Occupational Licensing," *British Journal of Industrial Relations* 48, no. 4 (2010): 676–687.

21. Rajan and Zingales argue that large incumbent firms invest in political influence in order to lock in the status quo, which preserves their dominance. Raghuram Rajan and Luigi Zingales, *Saving Capitalism From the Capitalists: Unleashing the Power of Financial Markets to Create Wealth and Spread Opportunity* (New York: Crown Business, 2003).

22. George Stigler, "The Theory of Economic Regulation," *Bell Journal of Economics and Management Science* 2, (1971): 3–21.

supposed to regulate. While the commission had been created to force railroad shipping rates down, railway men soon found that they could influence the commission and get it to force prices above what the competitive market would bear.[23] In 1892, U.S. Attorney General Richard Olney explained this point to his former employer, a railway boss:

> The Commission. . . is, or can be made, of great use to the railroads. It satisfies the popular clamor for a government supervision of the railroads, at the same time that that supervision is almost entirely nominal. Further, the older such a commission gets to be, the more inclined it will be found to take the business and railroad view of things. . . . The part of wisdom is not to destroy the Commission, but to utilize it.[24]

As the ICC case makes clear, regulations can be especially useful to firms if they give the *appearance* of being anti-business or somehow pro-consumer. Regulations are often supported by strange bedfellows. Bruce Yandle of Clemson University has studied the phenomenon extensively:

> The pages of history are full of episodes best explained by a theory of regulation I call "bootleggers and Baptists." Bootleggers. . . support Sunday closing laws that shut down all the local bars and liquor stores. Baptists support the same laws and lobby vigorously for them. Both parties gain, while the regulators are content because the law is easy to administer.[25]

23. Milton Friedman and Rose Friedman, *Free to Choose: A Personal Statement* (New York: Harcourt Brace Janovich, 1980), 194–203.

24. Ibid., 197.

25. Bruce Yandle, "Bootleggers and Baptists: The Education of a Regulatory Economist," Regulation 3, no. 3 (May/June 1983): 12–16.

The moralizing arguments are often front and center in regulatory policy debates, while the narrow interests that stand to benefit from certain regulations are much less conspicuous.

C. Subsidies

Some privileges are more obvious. In the last 10 years, the federal government has transferred over $191 billion in subsidies to farmers and the owners of farmland.[26] These benefits are directed toward a relatively small number of producers. According to an Environmental Working Group analysis of USDA data, just 10 percent of U.S. farms collect 74 percent of subsidy payments while 62 percent of farms receive no direct payments at all.[27] Agricultural subsidies are often characterized as a safety net for poor farmers. But in 2008, the last year for which data were available, the average household income of farms receiving $30,000 or more in subsidies was $210,000.[28] The agricultural industry is the largest beneficiary of direct subsidization, but other industries are privileged as well. The energy industry, for example, received more than $14 billion in direct subsidies in FY2010 (in addition to indirect subsidies such as tax privileges, discussed below).[29]

D. Loan Guarantees

A number of firms and industries receive indirect support through loan guarantees or through subsidies given to their customers.

26. Office of Management and Budget, *Historical Tables*, Table 3.2, budget function 351. In addition to these direct transfers, the government has spent another $50 billion subsidizing crop insurance and marketing for various agricultural products. See budget function 352.

27. Environmental Working Group, *2011 Farm Subsidy Database* (Washington, DC: EWG, 2012).

28. Ibid.

29. U.S. Energy Information Administration, *Direct Federal Financial Interventions and Subsidies in Energy in Fiscal Year 2010*, Table 10 (Washington, DC: U.S. Department of Energy, July 2011), http://www.eia.gov/analysis/requests/subsidy/pdf/subsidy.pdf.

In 2009, the energy firm Solyndra received $535 million in loan guarantees from the federal government. If the firm succeeded, it would repay its debt; if it failed, taxpayers would pick up the tab. Just two years later, the firm filed for bankruptcy, laying off its 1,100 employees and leaving taxpayers with the cost of the loan. The case has garnered a great deal of attention because there is evidence the White House rushed the approval process so that Vice President Joe Biden could announce the deal at a groundbreaking ceremony for the company's factory.[30]

But Solyndra is not alone in receiving special treatment. Since its inception in 2005, dozens of firms have taken advantage of the Energy Department's loan guarantee program.[31] And similar loan guarantee programs are administered by the Export-Import Bank, the Small Business Administration, and the Department of Agriculture. The Export-Import Bank, for example, offers loan guarantees to airlines that are customers of Boeing.[32]

E. Tax Privileges

In 1773, the British Parliament voted for a tax cut and the American colonies erupted in protest. The problem—from the perspective of the original Tea Party patriots—was that the tax cut applied to just one firm: the East India Company. The company was the largest government-sponsored enterprise of its day, benefiting from a number of perquisites including a government charter and a monopoly on trade in the East.[33] But the tax cut added one

---

30. Joe Stephens and Carol Leonnig, "Solyndra Loan: White House Pressed on Review of Solar Company Now Under Investigation," *Washington Post*, September 13, 2011.

31. U.S. Department of Energy Loan Programs Office, http://loanprograms.energy.gov/ (accessed May 3, 2012).

32. Air India, for example, has been a big beneficiary. Air India's competitor, Delta, has complained vociferously. Zachary A. Goldfarb, "Obama's Support for Export Industry Leads to Clash of U.S. Interests," *Washington Post*, February 18, 2012.

33. Like the so-called government-sponsored enterprises of our time—Fannie Mae and Freddie Mac—the government charter implied that the firm was backed by the full faith and credit of the British government.

more privilege. Since American merchants would continue to pay duties on tea that did not pass through Britain or the company, the act threatened to give the company a monopoly on the tea trade in America.[34]

Today, thousands of U.S. companies benefit from special provisions in both federal and state tax codes that offer "targeted tax relief" to particular firms or industries. Film production companies operating in the state of Virginia, for example, pay no sales tax on production-related products and are allowed refundable individual and corporate income tax credits. Thirty-nine other states offer similar special treatment to film production companies.[35] Manufacturers also benefit from a federal tax credit that allows them to reduce their tax liability. The credit isn't available to nonmanufacturing businesses such as health care, education, or entertainment companies. Since targeted tax breaks are often no more than subsidies in disguise, policy experts refer to them as "tax expenditures."[36]

F. Bailouts

In 1971, the United States government, for the first time in its nearly 200-year history, bailed out a single firm.[37] The firm was Lockheed Aircraft Corporation, and the bailout took the form of $250 million in emergency loan guarantees.[38] Three years later,

34. Edward Countryman, *The American Revolution* (New York: Hill and Wang, 1985), 52–56.

35. In addition to these tax subsidies, production companies may also receive grants from the state. See Virginia Film Office, "Incentives," http://www.film.virginia.org/incentives/ (accessed March 30, 2012). For a tally of all state film tax credits, see Mark Robyn and I. Harry David, "Movie Production Incentives in the Last Frontier," *Tax Foundation Special Report* 199 (April 2012).

36. Jason Fichtner and Jacob Feldman, "When Are Tax Expenditures Really Spending? A Look at Tax Expenditures and Lessons from the Tax Reform Act of 1986" (working paper, Mercatus Center at George Mason University, Arlington, VA, 2011).

37. Barry Ritholtz, *Bailout Nation: How Greed and Easy Money Corrupted Wall Street and Shook the World Economy* (Hoboken, NJ: Wiley, 2009), 34.

38. Ibid.

Penn Central Railroad received $676 million in loan guarantees.[39] Then, in the winter of 1979–80, Congress passed and President Carter signed the Chrysler Corporation Loan Guarantee Act.[40] With that, the government cosigned a $1.5 billion emergency loan package for the nation's third-largest auto manufacturer. In 1984, the Federal Deposit Insurance Corporation rescued the creditors of Continental Illinois National Bank and Trust Company. This bailout marked the first application of the theory that some firms—or at least their creditors—are "too big to fail."[41] Next, taxpayers saved the creditors of hundreds of savings and loan (S&L) associations in the S&L crisis of the early 1990s. This cost taxpayers almost $179 billion.[42] In the late 1990s, the Fed orchestrated the private bailout of hedge fund Long-Term Capital Management. This time, no taxpayer money was involved. But the Fed's keen interest in the case led many industry observers to believe that the Fed would not let large institutions—or their creditors—fail.[43]

One decade later there would be a spasm of bailouts: first the New York Federal Reserve made a $30 billion loan to J.P. Morgan Chase so that it could purchase Bear Stearns. Next, in order to save them from bankruptcy, the federal government took over mortgage giants Fannie Mae and Freddie Mac. Then the government paused, allowing Lehman Brothers and its creditors to fall on September 15, 2008. Two days later, bailouts resumed and the Federal Reserve made an $85 billion loan to the insurance firm American International Group. This bailout ultimately topped $173 billion. The culmination of this series of bailouts was the Troubled Asset Relief Program (TARP), a $700 billion bailout that

39. Ibid, 11.

40. *Chrysler Corporation Loan Guarantee Act of 1979*, Public Law No. 96-185, *U.S. Statutes at Large* 93 (1980): 1324.

41. Ritholtz, *Bailout Nation*, 212.

42. Ibid, 11

43. Luigi Zingales, *A Capitalism for the People: Recapturing the Lost Genius of American Prosperity* (Philadelphia, PA: Basic Books, 2012), 58.

gave hundreds of financial firms and auto companies emergency government assistance.[44]

G. Expected Bailouts

Well before they were rescued by the federal government, Fannie Mae and Freddie Mac benefited from the *expectation* of government assistance. The firms were chartered by Congress and widely assumed to have its financial support. This assumption meant that compared with firms lacking support from the federal government, Fannie and Freddie appeared to be safer investments. This expectation, in turn, allowed the companies to obtain loans at interest rates fully one half of one percent lower than their competitors—a major competitive edge.[45] The federal government's history of bailing out creditors made this expectation particularly strong.[46]

H. Tariffs and Quotas on Foreign Competition

For much of American history, trade barriers have historically been a significant—perhaps the dominant—source of privilege.[47] But in a remarkable triumph of economic evidence over special-interest pleading (the vast majority of economists oppose trade barriers), tariffs have steadily fallen throughout the course of the twentieth century.[48] The average tax on dutiable imports peaked

44. See Reports and Audits, *Office of the Special Inspector General for the Troubled Asset Relief Program*, http://www.sigtarp.gov/pages/reportsaudits.aspx.

45. Gretchen Morgenson and Joshua Rosner, *Reckless Endangerment: How Outsized Ambition, Greed, and Corruption Led to Economic Armageddon* (New York: Times Books, 2011), 16.

46. Barry Ritholtz, "Ritholtz on Bailouts, the Fed, and the Crisis," *EconTalk*, March 1, 2010.

47. Jeffrey Rogers Hummel, "The Civil War and Reconstruction," in *Government and the American Economy: A New History*, ed. Price Fishback (Chicago: University of Chicago Press, 2007).

48. On economists' views of trade, see Robert Whaples, "Do Economists Agree on Anything? Yes!" *Economists' Voice* 3, no. 9 (November 2006): 1–6.

at 59 percent in 1932 and steadily fell to 4.84 percent in the year 2000 (the last year for which comparable data were available).[49]

Two exceptions to this decline are noteworthy: on April 1, 1983, the Reagan administration broke with its stated preference for free trade and, in response to a petition from Harley-Davidson, imposed tariffs of up to 49.4 percent on imported heavyweight motorcycles.[50] Nearly two decades later, the George W. Bush administration would impose tariffs ranging from 8 to 30 percent on foreign producers of steel.

Other barriers to trade, such as import quotas, anti-dumping laws, exchange-rate manipulation, and direct or indirect subsidies, also privilege certain domestic firms. As tariffs have come down, such policies may have become a more important source of privilege for certain firms.

I. Noncompetitive Bidding

When President Dwight Eisenhower warned against the "unwarranted influence" of the "military-industrial complex," he was concerned that certain firms selling to the government might obtain untoward privilege.[51] It is telling that one of those contractors, Lockheed Aircraft, was the first bailout recipient.

A century later, accusations would fly that the George W. Bush administration's "no-bid" contracts to Halliburton and Blackwater were just the sort of nefarious deals that Eisenhower had warned of.[52] It is true that the firms were awarded contracts

49. Douglas Irwin, "Table Ee424-430 – Merchandise Imports and Duties: 1790–2000," in *Historical Statistics of the United States: Millennial Edition Online* (Cambridge University Press, 2012).

50. Daniel Klein, "Taking America for a Ride: The Politics of Motorcycle Tariffs," *Cato Policy Analysis* 32 (1984).

51. Dwight D. Eisenhower, "Military-Industrial Complex Speech, 1961," in *The Avalon Project: Documents in Law, History, and Diplomacy,* Yale Law School, http://avalon.law.yale.edu/20th_century/eisenhower001.asp (accessed March 30, 2012).

52. See, for example, Dan Briody, *The Halliburton Agenda: The Politics of Oil and Money* (Hoboken, NJ: Wiley, 2004).

that did not go out to open bidding. But it is also true that federal regulations explicitly permit such sole-source contracts in certain circumstances, such as when only one firm is capable of providing a certain service, when there is an unusual or compelling emergency, or when national security is at stake.[53] Also, had the government *not* contracted with these private firms, a government agency would have performed the service. In this case the agency itself would be a privileged monopolist.[54] These examples highlight the point that not all privileges are clear cut. Sometimes contracts are awarded by cronyism. Sometimes they are awarded by merit. It is not always easy to tell the difference.

J. Multiple Privileges

The list of categories of privilege above is not exhaustive. Moreover, none of the species of privilege I have listed are mutually exclusive. For example, in addition to the lower borrowing costs that attended its implicit (and then explicit) bailout guarantee, Fannie Mae also enjoyed a line of credit at the U.S. Treasury, an exemption from state and local taxes, an exemption from Securities and Exchange Commission filing requirements, and lower capital requirements (while regulations required other firms to have at least $10 of shareholder equity backing every $100 of mortgages on their books, Fannie only needed to have $2.50 in shareholder funds for every $100 in mortgages and could borrow the rest).[55]

---

53. *Code of Federal Regulations*, title 48, chapter 1, part 6.302.

54. A large economic literature models government agencies as monopolists selling services to elected officials. See William Niskanen, *Bureaucracy and Representative Government* (Chicago: Aldine-Atherton, 1971).

55. Morgenson and Rosner, *Reckless Endangerment*, 16 and 28.

III. THE ECONOMIC AND SOCIAL COSTS OF PRIVILEGE

There are a number of economic and social costs associated with privilege, and I will discuss each in turn. To motivate the discussion, assume that a firm has been granted an exclusive monopoly right: by law, no other firms are allowed to compete with it. From the firm's perspective, this privilege is particularly profitable; from society's perspective, it is particularly costly. But *all* of the varieties of privilege described above entail some degree of monopoly power and all are susceptible to the sorts of problems described herein.

A. Monopoly Costs

In the ideal competitive market described in section I, individual firms are said to be "price takers" because they must accept the price that prevails in the overall market. If they set their prices above this prevailing market price, their customers will turn to other sellers. And because competitive pressures tend to push the market price toward the marginal cost of production, if they set their prices below the market level, they will lose money and might even go out of business. In such a market, the profits of any one firm are modest (economists call these "normal profits").

In the short run, however, firms may be able to earn above-normal profits by either finding innovative ways to lower their costs or by differentiating their products from those of their competitors with improvements in quality that allow them to charge a higher price. In a free and open market, the innovative firms will soon be imitated by other firms who will enter the market and bid the price back down to competitive levels.

This process is known as "monopolistic competition" because firms are constantly pushing to differentiate themselves from their competitors and gain some degree of monopoly pricing power.[56]

---

56. Edward Chamberlain, *The Theory of Monopolistic Competition: A Reorientation of the Theory of Value* (Cambridge, MA: Harvard University Press, 1933).

This type of market structure is in some ways ideal: in the short run, the lure of monopoly profit encourages innovation, while in the long run, the discipline of an open market keeps prices low. Thus, firms that fail to innovate or fail to economize on cost will eventually be driven out of the industry. But the key to the process is open entry and exit. New firms must be allowed to enter the industry and compete; old firms that fail to innovate and provide value to customers must be forced to shutter their doors. In this way, open entry and exit discipline the industry to focus on maximizing consumer benefits while minimizing production costs.

When a government grants one firm a monopoly, however, there is no discipline. The firm will possess pricing power that a competitive firm lacks. It need not accept the price that would emerge in a competitive market and is instead said to be a "price maker." If the firm is interested in maximizing its profit, it will set a higher price than that which would prevail in a competitive industry.

There are five obvious implications of monopoly (and some not-so-obvious ones, as we will see in the following sections). First, a monopoly firm gains more from exchange than it would were it a competitive firm. This is because it captures the entire market and charges that market a higher price than a competitive firm would. Second, consumers still gain from exchange, but they gain less than they would were the market subject to free entry by competitors. Third, would-be competitors—those not blessed with monopoly privilege—lose out on the opportunity to gain from exchange. Fourth, total sales under monopoly are less than total sales under competition because the higher price drives some customers out of the market. Finally, the monopolist's gains are less than the losses of consumers and would-be producers. Hence, society as a whole is worse off under monopoly than under competition (see figure 2 in the appendix, on page 41, for a fuller explanation).

Economists refer to these social costs as the "deadweight loss" of monopoly. Under monopoly, there are mutually beneficial trades that could occur, but do not. It is estimated that each year, monopolies cost Americans between $60 billion and $240 billion in deadweight costs.[57]

B. Productive Inefficiencies (*X*-Inefficiency)

Deadweight losses are not the only costs associated with a government-granted monopoly. Shielded from the discipline of a competitive market, managers and workers at monopolistic firms may exert less effort and may be less efficient than they would be under competitive circumstances. This insight was first developed by economist Harvey Leibenstein. To distinguish this type of inefficiency from other types, such as traditional deadweight loss, he called it "*X*-inefficiency."[58]

Leibenstein noted that in most circumstances, individuals and firms are not as efficient as economists' models assume. There is always room for "slack." And when firms are protected from competition, there will tend to be more slack. He writes, "For a variety of reasons people and organizations normally work neither as hard or as effectively as they could. In situations where competitive pressure is light, many people will trade the disutility of greater effort, or search for the utility of feeling less pressure and of better interpersonal relations."[59]

Thus, due to workers' diminished efforts, marginal production costs in an *X*-inefficient firm will be greater than those of a competitive firm (see figure 3 in the appendix, on page 42, for more details). The firm will also sell less, consumers will gain less from exchange, and the deadweight loss of monopoly will be larger.

57. John Taylor and Akila Weerapana, *Principles of Microeconomics: Global Financial Crisis Edition* (Mason, OH: South-Western Cengage Learning, 2010), 285–286.

58. Harvey Leibenstein, "Allocative Efficiency vs. 'X-Efficiency,'" *American Economic Review* 56, no. 3 (June 1966): 392–415.

59. Ibid., 413.

The USPS is a classic example of X-inefficiency. While USPS must compete with private firms in package and urgent delivery services, its monopoly status in the areas where it does not face competition, such as nonurgent deliveries, seems to have made the USPS inefficient. Postage prices offer evidence of this inefficiency. While most goods tend to get cheaper in inflation-adjusted terms over time, the price of a first-class stamp rose by twice the rate of inflation from 1970 to 2010.[60]

C. Inattention to Consumer Desires

Protected firms are not only unlikely to minimize costs; they are also unlikely to maximize consumer benefits. In other words, they will be less attentive to consumer desires and will tend to produce lower-quality products. Thus, X-inefficiency may result in both increased marginal costs *and* decreased consumer benefits.[61] Because consumers will derive less value from each unit they buy, they will not demand as much of the product and the firm will sell less than it otherwise would.

Here, again, the USPS is illustrative. Not only does the firm have trouble containing costs; it also has trouble maintaining quality. Packages shipped via USPS are more likely to break than those shipped via the United Parcel Service (UPS).[62] And when Hurricane Katrina struck, the private shippers UPS, FedEx, and DHL all restored service to New Orleans within weeks, while the USPS took seven months to reopen its processing and distribution center.[63]

60. William McEachern, *Microeconomics: A Contemporary Introduction*, 9th ed. (Mason, OH: South-Western Cengage Learning, 2012), 217.

61. In an influential paper, Michael Mussa and Sherwin Rosen show that a "monopolist almost always reduces the quality sold to any customer compared with what would be purchased under competition" (p. 301). To my knowledge, however, no one has explored the link between X-inefficiency and decreased consumer benefits. See Mussa and Rosen, "Monopoly and Product Quality, *Journal of Economic Theory* 18 (1978): 301–317.

62. McEachern, *Microeconomics*, 217.

63. Ibid.

D. Rent-Seeking

As we have seen, privilege is costly for society at large but, at least for a time, it can be quite lucrative for those fortunate enough to obtain government favors. Economists refer to the above-normal profits of a privileged firm as "rent."[64] And because rents can be substantial, firms are willing to go to some effort to obtain and maintain them. Firms will donate to political campaigns and political action committees, sponsor advertisements designed to sway public policy, maintain expensive lobbying operations in state and national capitols, and go to great lengths to curry favor with politicians. Even those firms that do not seek their own privileges may invest heavily in political activities in order to fend off attempts by competitors to obtain their own privileges.

Economists refer to these activities as "rent-seeking."[65] Because rent-seeking requires resources—time, money, and effort—and because it creates no value for consumers, it is another social cost of government-granted privilege. The amount of money wasted in rent-seeking depends on the value of the rent. The more valuable the privilege, the more resources will be wasted in rent-seeking. The amount lost also depends on the returns to political activity. For example, it may be the case that the more a firm plays politics, the better it gets at the game. In this case, economists have shown that the total cost of all efforts to obtain rent, maintain rent, or fend off a competitor's attempts to rent-seek can exceed the total value of the rent itself.[66] Though no one firm would rationally spend more to obtain a privilege than the privilege is worth, the sum of

64. Classical economist David Ricardo was the first to introduce the term. It has no relation to the word "rent" as it is normally used in English.

65. Gordon Tullock developed the concept in 1967, and Anne Krueger introduced the term in 1974. See Tullock, "The Welfare Costs of Tariffs, Monopolies and Theft," *Western Economic Journal* 5 (1967): 224–232; Anne Krueger, "The Political Economy of the Rent-Seeking Society," *American Economic Review* 64 (1974): 291–303.

66. "Overdissipation" is the term for this scenario. For details, see Dennis Mueller, *Public Choice III* (New York: Cambridge University Press, 2003), 336–337. On the possibility of increasing returns to rent-seeking, see Kevin Murphy, Andrei Shleifer, and Robert Vishny, "Why Is Rent-Seeking So Costly to Growth?" *American Economic Review Papers and Proceedings* 83, no. 2 (1993): 409–414.

all firms' efforts may be greater than the value of the privilege. There have been a number of attempts to measure the aggregate social cost of rent-seeking. These studies suggest that the annual cost is somewhere between 7 percent and 22.6 percent of gross national output.[67] For the U.S. economy, this means the annual cost may range from $1 to $3.5 trillion.

E. Distributional Effects

Before moving on to discuss some of the other implications of privilege, it is important to emphasize that monopoly privileges create winners and losers. The owners and operators of the monopoly firm, of course, win. They capture the entire market and charge it a high price. Unlike the owners and operators of competitive firms, monopolists need not worry about competition. As the economist John Hicks once put it, "the best of all monopoly profits is a quiet life."[68] Those who help monopolists obtain rent also win: lobbyists and political consultants can command impressive salaries because their connections are worth it.

On the losing side are the consumers and would-be competitors. Consumers pay higher prices for low-quality goods. And would-be competitors are unable to reap any gains from exchange. Economists often emphasize that the losers lose more than the winners win (see the appendix for details). This outcome explains why economists consider monopoly to be inefficient. But for many people, it may be just as important to note that the winners are more likely to be wealthy and well-connected than the losers. This disparity may explain why both the Tea Party and the Occupy Wall Street movements opposed the Wall Street bailouts.

67. Keith Cowling and Dennis Mueller, "The Social Costs of Monopoly Power," *Economic Journal* 88 (1978): 727–748; Richard Posner, "The Social Cost of Monopoly and Regulation," *Journal of Political Economy* 83 (1975): 807–827; Krueger, "The Political Economy of the Rent-Seeking Society"; and David Laband and John Sophocleus, "The Social Cost of Rent-Seeking: First Estimates," *Public Choice* 58 (1988): 269–275.

68. J. R. Hicks, "Annual Survey of Economic Theory: The Theory of Monopoly," *Econometrica* 3, no. 1 (January 1935): 8.

F. Unproductive Entrepreneurship

Joseph Schumpeter is credited with highlighting the key role of entrepreneurship in economics. The entrepreneur's function, he wrote, is to "reform or revolutionize the pattern of production."[69] The entrepreneur does this by developing new goods and new production methods, by opening new markets and exploiting previously unused resources, and by developing new ways to organize firms.[70] More recently, however, economists have come to realize that entrepreneurs may innovate in socially unproductive ways as well. New York University economist William Baumol is credited with this insight. According to Baumol, there is such a thing as unproductive entrepreneurship. "Schumpeter's list of entrepreneurial activities" Baumol writes, "can usefully be expanded to include such items as innovations in rent-seeking procedures, for example, discovery of a previously unused legal gambit that is effective in diverting rents to those who are first in exploiting it."[71] Baumol hypothesizes that when governments hand out rents, talented people will be less likely to engage in productive entrepreneurism and more likely to engage in unproductive or even destructive entrepreneurism that results in the destruction of wealth.

Similarly, economists Kevin Murphy, Andrei Shleifer, and Robert Vishny note that a country's "most talented people" can organize production in two different ways.[72] On the one hand, they may "start [or improve] firms," in which case they will "innovate and foster growth." On the other hand, they may "become

69. Joseph Schumpeter, *Capitalism, Socialism, and Democracy* (New York: Harper & Brothers, [1942] 1950), 132.

70. Joseph Schumpeter, *The Theory of Economic Development* (Leipzig: Duncker and Humblot, [1912] 1934), 66.

71. William Baumol, "Entrepreneurship: Productive, Unproductive, and Destructive," *The Journal of Political Economy* 98, no. 5, part 1 (October 1990): 893–921, 897.

72. Kevin Murphy, Andrei Shleifer, and Robert Vishny, "The Allocation of Talent: Implications for Growth," *Quarterly Journal of Economics* 106, no. 2 (May 1991): 503–530.

rent seekers," in which case, "they only redistribute wealth and reduce growth."[73]

Think of the thousands of talented lawyers, lobbyists, and strategic thinkers who occupy the expensive office buildings lining K Street in Washington, D.C. All of this talent might be employed in the discovery of new ways to bring value to consumers and to expand the gains from exchange. Instead, many of these smart and hardworking people spend their time convincing politicians to hand out privileges to their own firms or fending off attempts to hand out privileges to their competitors.

Empirical tests support the theory of unproductive entrepreneurship. Economists Russell Sobel of West Virginia University and Thomas Garrett of Kansas State University have developed a number of measures of unproductive entrepreneurial activity based on the concentration of political and lobbying organizations in state capitals.[74] Using these measures, Sobel has found that those states in which privileges are more likely to be dispensed (as indicated by a low level of economic freedom) tend to have higher levels of unproductive entrepreneurship and lower levels of productive entrepreneurship.[75]

Other research suggests that unproductive entrepreneurship is associated with slower economic growth. Murphy, Shleifer, and Vishny, for example, studied this question using data from 55 countries. As a proxy for productive entrepreneurism, they used the proportion of college students majoring in engineering. And as a proxy for unproductive entrepreneurism, they used the proportion of students concentrating in law. Up to a certain point, lawyers are theoretically good for growth; they help delineate and define property rights and they help maintain the rule of law. But beyond some minimum point, more lawyers may lead to more

73. Ibid.

74. Russell Sobel and Thomas Garrett, "On the Measurement of Rent Seeking and Its Social Opportunity Cost," *Public Choice* 112 (2002): 115–136.

75. Russell Sobel, "Testing Baumol: Institutional Quality and the Productivity of Entrepreneurship," *Journal of Business Venturing* 23 (2008): 641–655.

rent-seeking. Even if lawyers themselves are not the cause of rent seeking, they may be an indication of it. In the same way that a large number of police per capita may be an indication of a city's inherent violence, a large number of lawyers per capita may be an indication of a nation's tendency to rent-seek.

In their analysis of the data, the authors found that a 10 percentage point increase in the share of students concentrating in law was associated with 0.78 percent slower annual growth in per capita GDP.[76] This can add up over time. In 2010, per capita GDP was about 65 percent greater than it was in 1980. But if the economy had grown 0.78 percent slower over that same period, per capita GDP in 2010 would only be 30 percent greater than it was in 1980.[77]

G. Loss of Innovation and Diminished Long-Run Economic Growth

Privilege can also have a profoundly negative effect on innovation. And a lack of innovation, in turn, can disadvantage an entire society. For example, economist Chun-Lei Yang has shown that as rent-seeking activities grow more prevalent, firms have less of an incentive to invest in productivity-enhancing research and development. Thus, privileged firms are less likely to innovate.[78]

Empirical research supports this claim. For example, economists Stefanie Lenway, Randall Morck, and Bernard Yeung studied a decade's worth of data from 130 steel firms to look for differences between firms that lobby heavily and those that do not. They found that the most active lobbyers "tend to be larger,

---

76. Murphy, Shleifer, and Vishny, "The Allocation of Talent," 526.

77. Author's calculations based on Census population estimates and BEA data. See Bureau of Economic Analysis, *Current Dollar and 'Real' GDP* (Washington, DC: U.S. Department of Commerce, 2012) and U.S. Census Bureau, *Population and Housing Unit Estimates* (Washington, DC: U.S. Department of Commerce, 2012).

78. Chung-Lei Yang, "Rent Seeking, Technology Commitment, and Economic Development," *Journal of Institutional and Theoretical Economics* 154, no. 4 (December 1998): 640–658.

older, less diversified, and less profitable than non-lobbyers" and concluded that protection "appears to reward less innovative firms."[79] International evidence supports the claim that firms that are more likely to ask for privilege tend to be less profitable. In a survey of 450 politically connected firms from 35 countries, Mara Faccio, Ronald Masulis, and John McConnell concluded that "among bailed-out firms, those that are politically connected exhibit significantly worse financial performance than their non-connected peers at the time of and following the bailout."[80]

As protected firms become less innovative, a country's overall economic growth may suffer. This is because, as Schumpeter emphasized nearly a century ago, economic growth thrives on "creative destruction." In a healthy economy, new firms constantly arise to challenge older, less-innovative behemoths.[81] One of the leading experts on entrepreneurship, Amar Bhidé of the Columbia Business School, has argued that big firms, encumbered by larger internal bureaucracies, are virtually incapable of capitalizing on radical ideas.[82] Indeed, research finds that new firms are more likely than existing firms to license novel technology.[83]

79. Stefanie Lenway, Randall Morck, and Bernard Yeung, "Rent Seeking, Protectionism and Innovation in the American Steel Industry," *The Economic Journal* 106 (March 1996): 410–421, 410.

80. Mara Faccio, Ronald Masulis, and John McConnell, "Political Connections and Corporate Bailouts," *Journal of Finance* 61, no. 6 (December 2006): 2597–2635, 2597.

81. Schumpeter, *Capitalism, Socialism and Democracy*. More recently, this argument has been formalized. See Philippe Aghion and Peter Howitt, "A Model of Growth Through Creative Destruction," *Econometrica* 60 (1992): 323–351, and Philippe Aghion and Peter Howitt, *Endogenous Growth Theory* (Cambridge, MA: MIT Press, 1998).

82. Amar Bhidé, "How Novelty Aversion Affects Financing Options," *Capitalism and Society* 1, no. 1 (2006): 1–31.

83. Scott Shane, "Technology Opportunities and New Firm Formation," *Management Science* 47, no. 2 (2001).

And compared with larger firms, smaller firms are about twice as likely to file "high-impact" patents.[84]

For these reasons, turnover among a nation's largest firms is a sign of vitality. The list of U.S. Fortune 500 companies is illustrative: Only 13.4 percent of those companies on the Fortune 500 list in 1955 were still there in 2010.[85] But not all nations experience the same sort of "churn" among their top firms. To test Schumpeter's theory, Kathy Fogel, Randall Morck, and Bernard Yeung recently examined the link between turnover among nations' top firms and economic growth.[86] They looked at the lists of top firms in 44 countries in 1975 and again in 1996. After controlling for other factors, they found that those nations with more turnover among their top firms tended to experience faster per capita economic growth, greater productivity growth, and faster capital growth. Looking at the factors that correlate with faster firm turnover, they found that "big business turnover also correlates with smaller government, common law, less bank-dependence, stronger shareholder rights, and greater openness [to trade]."[87] Thus, turnover is less likely when firms are priveleged.

In a classic, sweeping study, economist Mancur Olson went so far as to claim that special-interest privilege can account for the "rise and decline of nations."[88] As societies grow wealthy and stable, he argued, the seeds of their own destruction are sewn.

84. CHI Research, Inc., *Small Serial Innovators: The Small Firm Contribution in Technical Change*, prepared for the Small Business Administration's Office of Advocacy (Haddon Heights, NJ: CHI, 2003); Council on Competitiveness, *Innovate America* (Washington, D.C.: Council on Competitiveness, 2004); Zoltan Acs and David Audretsch, *Innovation and Small Firms* (Cambridge, MA: MIT Press, 1990).

85. Mark Perry, "Fortune 500 Firms in 1955 vs. 2011," *Carpe Diem* blog, November 23, 2011, http://mjperry.blogspot.com/2011/11/fortune-500-firms-in-1955-vs-2011-87.html.

86. Kathy Fogel, Randall Morck, and Bernard Yeung, "Big Business Stability and Economic Growth: Is What's Good for General Motors Good for America?" *Journal of Financial Economics* 89 (2008): 83–108.

87. Ibid., 83.

88. Mancur Olson, *The Rise and Decline of Nations: Economic Growth, Stagflation and Social Rigidities* (New York: Yale University Press, 1982).

Stable societies are fertile ground for special interests. These interest groups grow in power and influence over time, and once entrenched, rarely disappear. "On balance," they "reduce efficiency and aggregate income in the societies in which they operate and make political life more divisive." Eventually, "The accumulation of distributional coalitions [those that seek rents] increases the complexity of regulation, the role of government, and the complexity of understandings, and changes the direction of social evolution."[89]

Olson used his theory to explain the relative decline of the United Kingdom throughout the twentieth century. As a remarkably stable society, by 1982 the UK had accumulated large numbers of powerful, entrenched interest groups. These groups obtained various government privileges, which, in turn, slowed the UK's economic growth compared to that of other large, industrialized nations. In contrast, World War II and postwar reconstruction swept away the entrenched interests in Germany and Japan, allowing these countries to grow much faster than the UK. (In the 30 years since Olson's study, one might argue that powerful interest groups have again begun to ensnare Germany and Japan). Similarly, Olson found that the economies of those U.S. states that had been settled the longest tended to grow slower, presumably because they had accumulated a greater number of powerful special-interest groups.[90]

H. Macroeconomic Instability

In the previous section, I discussed the ways in which government-granted privilege can undermine long-run economic

---

89. Ibid., 74.

90. A large literature has evolved to test Olson's central hypothesis. Jac Heckelman recently reviewed 50 studies in this literature. He found that "on the whole, the theory of institutional sclerosis is generally but certainly not universally supported." Heckelman, "*Explaining the Rain: The Rise and Decline of Nations After 25 Years,*" *Southern Economic Journal* 74, no. 1 (2007): 18–33.

growth. For a number of reasons, privilege may also undermine short-run macroeconomic stability.

For one thing, government privilege often encourages undue risk-taking. The problem is especially acute when gains are privatized while losses are socialized (for example, through a bailout or the promise of a bailout). The economic term for this behavior is "moral hazard." It refers to the tendency for individuals to take on undue risk when they know they will not bear the full costs of failure.

A group of economists at the International Monetary Fund (IMF) recently studied this problem and its contribution to the 2008 financial crisis.[91] They looked at data from nearly 9,000 lenders in 378 U.S. metropolitan areas spanning the years 1999 to 2007. They found that those lenders that lobbied more intensively tended to take on more risk as characterized by higher loan-to-income ratios, more securitization, and faster credit expansion. When the crisis hit, delinquency rates were higher in those areas where lobbying lenders aggressively expanded their lending practices, causing these lenders to suffer abnormally large losses during the crisis. The implication is clear: those lenders that lobbied more intensely (other things being equal) were more likely to be bailed out than their counterparts. As a result, the heavy lobbyers took on more undue risk. Thus, the true costs of a bailout like TARP encompasses more than the opportunity cost of taxpayer money paid to the failing company. It also includes the cost of the moral hazard it induces.

Privilege can also induce undue risk if it makes it more difficult for market participants to identify and learn from their mistakes. Financial economist and risk expert Nassim Taleb has explored this phenomenon in a number of works.[92] In a paper coauthored with political scientist Mark Blyth, he explained,

91. Deniz Igan, Prachi Mishra, and Thierry Tressel, "A Fistful of Dollars: Lobbying and the Financial Crisis" (working paper, International Monetary Fund, Washington, DC, 2009).

92. See, for example, Nassim Nicholas Taleb, *The Black Swan: The Impact of the Highly Improbable* (New York: Random House, 2007).

Complex systems that have artificially suppressed volatility tend to become extremely fragile, while at the same time exhibiting no visible risks. In fact, they tend to be too calm and exhibit minimal variability as silent risks accumulate beneath the surface. Although the stated intention of political leaders and economic policymakers is to stabilize the system by inhibiting fluctuations, the result tends to be the opposite.[93]

Even when privilege does not lead to excessive, undue risk-taking, it can still lead to instability by misallocating resources. When governments dispense privileges, the basic building blocks of growth—labor and capital—tend to be allocated on the basis of political considerations rather than on the basis of fundamental costs and benefits. This misallocation can lead to large and painful adjustments when the political considerations fail to coincide with market fundamentals.[94]

A number of economists have argued that political cronyism caused or at least exacerbated the financial crisis that rippled through many Asian economies in 1997. Indeed, the term "crony capitalism" was first popularized during this crisis.[95] In a study measuring the value of political connections in Indonesia, for example, Raymond Fisman of Columbia University stated a well-known hypothesis for the 1997 crisis: "The claim was that in Southeast Asia, political connectedness, rather than fundamentals

93. Nassim Taleb and Mark Blyth, "The Black Swan of Cairo: How Suppressing Volatility Makes the World Less Predictable and More Dangerous," *Foreign Affairs* 90, no. 3 (2011): 33–39. Taleb is currently working on a book that will elaborate on this point.

94. Arnold Kling has argued that economies are constantly adjusting to new circumstances, often brought on by technological change. "Unemployment fluctuations," he argues, are "a reflection of the difficulty that markets sometimes have in making the necessary adjustments." See Kling, "PSST: Patterns of Sustainable Specialization and Trade," *Capitalism and Society* 6, no. 2 (2011): 1–18.

95. Raghuram G. Rajan and Luigi Zingales, "Which Capitalism? Lessons from the East Asian Crisis," *Journal of Applied Corporate Finance* 2, no. 3 (fall 1998): 40-8.

such as productivity, was the primary determinant of profitability and that this had led to distorted investment decisions."[96] Fisman's analysis confirms that politically connected firms were particularly sensitive to changes in the health of their benefactor, President Suharto, and when the crisis hit, these firms suffered more than their unconnected counterparts.

William Baumol, Robert Litan, and Carl Schramm of the Kauffman Foundation describe a similar dynamic in South Korea:

> Long accustomed to directing its banks to provide loans to the larger South Korean conglomerates ("chaebols"), South Korea's government induced too many banks to invest excessively in the expansion of the semiconductor, steel, and chemicals industries. When the financial crisis that began in Southeast Asia during the summer of 1997 spread to South Korea, the country's banks and, more important, the companies that had borrowed to expand were so overextended that the South Korean economy came close to collapse.[97]

As often happens with privilege, the "solution" to this problem involved more privilege: South Korea was rescued by a U.S.-led effort to prop up South Korean financial institutions.[98] Baumol, Litan, and Schramm document similar problems in China and Japan.[99]

But we need not look so far for examples. Atif Mian of the University of California at Berkeley and Amir Sufi and Francesco

96. Raymond Fisman, "Estimating the Value of Political Connections," *The American Economic Review* 91, no. 4 (September 2001): 1095–1102.

97. William Baumol, Robert Litan, and Carl Schramm, *Good Capitalism, Bad Capitalism, and the Economics of Growth and Prosperity* (New Haven, CT: Yale University Press, 2007), 67–68. See also Stephan Haggard and Jongryn Mo, "The Political Economy of the Korean Financial Crisis," *Review of International Political Economy* 7, no. 2 (2000): 197–218.

98. Paul Bluestein, *The Chastening* (New York: Public Affairs, 2001).

99. Baumol, Litan, and Schramm, chapters 6 and 7.

Trebbi of the University of Chicago recently conducted an extensive examination of the political activity of the U.S. mortgage industry and housing interests in the run-up to the subprime meltdown of 2008.[100] The authors found, "Beginning in 2002, mortgage industry campaign contributions increasingly targeted U.S. representatives from districts with a large fraction of subprime borrowers." Analyzing more than 700 votes related to housing, the authors found that these contributions became an increasingly strong predictor of congressional votes. They also found that the share of constituents with low credit scores exerted increasing influence over voting patterns. Thus, "Pressure on the U.S. government to expand subprime credit came from both mortgage lenders and subprime borrowers."[101] Indeed, a slew of policies encouraged the expansion of credit in the subprime market. These policies, of course, benefited the privileged firms as well as the privileged subprime borrowers. But they also fanned the flames of an overheating housing market. For nearly a decade, capital and labor poured into housing and related industries, and when the bubble eventually burst, it threw the United States into its worst recession in decades.[102]

100. Atif Mian, Amier Sufi, and Francesco Trebbi, "The Political Economy of the Subprime Mortgage Credit Expansion" (National Bureau of Economic Research Working Paper Series no. 16107, Cambridge, MA, 2010).

101. Ibid., 23. The authors caution that "given the nature of political influence and the complexity of government decisions that affect mortgage markets, it is difficult to find a 'smoking gun' which shows with certainty the determinants of government policy. Our findings should therefore be viewed as suggestive evidence of the influence of subprime borrowers and lenders on policy." It should be noted, however, that theirs is not the only study to find such "suggestive evidence." See, for example, Atif Mian, Amir Sufi, and Francesco Trebbi, "The Political Economy of the U.S. Mortgage Default Crisis," *American Economic Review* 100, no. 5 (2010): 1967–1998. For a journalistic account, see Morgenson and Rosner, *Reckless Endangerment.*

102. The housing crisis is beyond the scope of this paper. There are, however, a number of good analyses of these events. See, for example, Arnold Kling, *Not What They Had in Mind: A History of Policies that Produced the Financial Crisis of 2008,* Mercatus Special Study (Arlington, VA: Mercatus Center at George Mason

I. Cronyism

Privilege entails cultural as well as economic costs. When governments dispense privileges, concerns of fairness and impartiality almost always arise. These concerns can undermine the legitimacy of both government and business, sometimes encouraging worse policy.

Objective criteria for dispensing privilege are hard to come by. Without objective standards, politicians may end up picking winners and losers on the basis of personal connections and political expediency. When they do, their reputations and those of the firms they favor suffer. Even when politicians try their best to be objective, those who dispense particular favors are almost always open to charges of nepotism or corruption. As the humorist P. J. O'Rourke once put it, "When buying and selling are controlled by legislation, the first things to be bought and sold are legislators."[103]

The data suggest these suspicions are well-founded. For example, the previously cited study by Faccio, Masulis, and McConnell found that politically connected firms were far more likely to be bailed out than similar firms without political connections.[104] A new study by Utah State University professors Benjamin Blau, Tyler Brough, and Diana Thomas offers further confirmation. They studied the lobbying expenditures and political activities of the 237 firms that received TARP funds. Controlling for other factors, they found that more intense lobbying and political activity made firms more likely to receive TARP funding, likely to receive

University, 2009). See also Peter J. Wallison, *Dissent from the Majority Report of the Financial Crisis Inquiry Commission* (Washington, DC: AEI Press, 2011); Raghuram Rajan, *Fault Lines: How Hidden Fractures Still Threaten the World Economy* (Princeton, NJ: Princeton University Press, 2011); Morgenson and Rosner, *Reckless Endangerment*. For a treatment that does not emphasize interest group politics, see John Taylor, *Getting Off Track: How Government Actions and Interventions Caused, Prolonged, and Worsened the Financial Crisis* (Stanford, CA: Hoover Institution Press, 2009).

103. Quoted in James Gwartney, Richard Stroup, Russell Sobel, and David Macpherson, *Macroeconomics: Private and Public Choice*, 13th ed. (Mason, OH: Cengage Learning, 2011), 136.

104. Faccio, Masulis, and McConnell, "Political Connections and Corporate Bailouts."

a larger amount of it, and more likely to receive it sooner. To be precise, they found that "for every dollar spent on lobbying during the five years before the TARP bailout, firms received between $485.77 and $585.65 in TARP support."[105]

The problem of cronyism is compounded by the phenomenon of the "revolving door," or the tendency for ex-government officials to find jobs in the industries they once oversaw and for industry insiders to find regulatory jobs overseeing their former colleagues. According to data from the Center for Responsive Politics, among those federal legislators who left office in 2010 and found new employment, nearly 33 percent went to work for lobbying firms and another 20 percent went to work for a major client of a lobbying firm.[106] Former Speaker of the House Newt Gingrich famously did some work for Freddie Mac after he left office in 1999. Between 1999 and 2007, Gingrich's firm received $1.6 million from the mortgage giant. According to the nonpartisan Congressional Budget Office, annual federal subsidies to the firm were about $4.6 billion during this time period.[107] The former speaker maintains that he was paid for his expertise and not for his connections.[108] But it is hard to believe that an equally knowledgeable person without his connections could command such a salary.

Indeed, research suggests that even after controlling for lobbyists' expertise, connections matter. Economists Jordi Blanes i Vidal, Mirko Draca, and Christian Fons-Rosen examined the political connections of over 7,000 firms. To isolate the influence of political connections on earnings, they looked at the change

105. Benjamin Blau, Tyler Brough, and Diana Thomas, "Corporate Lobbying, Political Connections, and the 2008 Troubled Asset Relief Program" (under review at the *Journal of Financial Economics*).

106. Center for Responsive Politics, "Revolving Door: Former Members of the 111th Congress," OpenSecrets.org, http://www.opensecrets.org/revolving/departing.php (accessed March 28, 2012).

107. Congressional Budget Office, *Federal Subsidies and the Housing GSEs*, May 2001.

108. Peter Overby, "Gingrich Fights Against the Lobbyist Label," *All Things Considered*, NPR, March 28, 2012.

in lobbyists' revenue after the departure of senators with whom they were connected. They found, "Lobbyists with experience in the office of a US Senator suffer a 24% drop in generated revenue when that Senator leaves office."[109] Similarly, a study by economists at MIT, Yale, and Brigham Young University looked at the value of political connections to Treasury Secretary Timothy Geithner. After controlling for other factors, they found, "The announcement of Timothy Geithner as President Barack Obama's nominee for Treasury Secretary in November 2008 produced a cumulative abnormal return for Geithner-connected financial firms of around 15 percent from day 0 (when the announcement was first leaked) to day 10."[110]

J. Diminished Legitimacy of Government and Business

The appearance of impropriety can have a profound effect on cultural perceptions of both business and government. University of Chicago economist Luigi Zingales, for example, argues that privileges sully the reputations of businesses and business leaders.[111] "The larger the share of capitalists who acquire their wealth thanks to their political connections," he avers, "the greater the

---

109. Jordi Blanes i Vidal, Mirko Draca, and Christian Fons-Rosen, "Revolving Door Lobbyists" (Centre for Economic Performance Discussion Paper no. 993, London School of Economics and Political Science, London, 2010), conditionally accepted by the *American Economic Review*.

110. Daron Acemoglu, Simon Johnson, Amir Kermani, James Kwak, and Todd Mitton, "The Value of Political Connections in the United States" (working paper, December 2011). Alarmingly, they note, "The quantitative effect is comparable to standard findings in emerging markets with weak institutions, and much higher than previous studies have found for the United States or other relatively rich democracies." For a previous study that found zero impact from political connections, see David Fisman, Ray Fisman, Julia Galef, and Rakesh Khurana, "Estimating the Value of Connections to Vice-President Cheney" (working paper, December 2005).

111. Luigi Zingales, "Capitalism After the Crisis," *National Affairs*, no. 1 (Fall 2009): 22–35.

perception that capitalism is unfair and corrupt."[112] The problem is increasingly evident in the U.S. financial sector, where,

> [I]ncreasing concentration and growing political muscle have undermined the traditional American understanding of the difference between free markets and big business. This means not only that the interests of finance now dominate the economic understanding of policymakers, but also—and perhaps more important— that the public's perception of the economic system's legitimacy is at risk.[113]

Zingales notes that other countries have gone down this path before. He cites the example of his birth country, Italy. There, businessman and (now former) Prime Minister Silvio Berlusconi "often seems to run the country in the interest of his media empire."[114] The melding of public and private interests has had a dramatic effect on public perception of the way to get ahead in Italy. Zingales writes, "When asked in a recent study to name the most important determinants of financial success, Italian managers put 'knowledge of influential people' in first place (80% considered it 'important' or 'very important'). 'Competence and experience' ranked fifth, behind characteristics such as 'loyalty and obedience.'"[115]

When business success becomes a function of who you know and not what you do for the customer, the public tends to look upon success with suspicion. Zingales points to international polls that suggest that compared to Brazilians, Danes, and Germans, a larger share of Americans believe that hard work rather than

---

112. Ibid., 26.

113. Ibid., 33.

114. Ibid., 28.

115. Ibid., 25; for the survey, see Primo Rapporto Luiss, *Generare Classe Dirigente: Un Percorso da Costruire* (Rome: Luiss University Press, 2007).

luck plays a major role in determining income differences.[116] This attitude, Zingales argues, explains why Americans have traditionally supported an open and free market. Things may be changing, however. In the years following the bailouts of hundreds of U.S. financial firms, public satisfaction with the size and influence of both business and government have plummeted. According to Gallup, public satisfaction with the federal government has fallen from a high of 60 percent in 2002 to a low of 29 percent in 2012, while satisfaction with "big business" has fallen from a high of 50 percent in 2002 to just 30 percent in 2012.[117]

In his work on entrepreneurship, economist William Baumol makes an argument similar to Zingales's.[118] Where Zingales believes that privilege may blur the distinction between productive and unproductive activity, Baumol hypothesizes that it may do more. In some cases, he argues, privilege may elevate unproductive activity to a higher cultural status than productive activity. He points to ancient Rome, where policies afforded plenty of opportunities to seek government privilege. While it was possible to gain wealth through productive entrepreneurship, Baumol argues that this choice was not the path to prestige. Productive activity such as commerce and industry tended to be the occupations of freed slaves for whom other, more prestigious, career paths were closed. Citing the noted classical scholar Moses Finley, Baumol argues that "persons of honorable status" resorted to other forms of "entrepreneurship." As Finley put it,

> The opportunity for "political moneymaking" can hardly be over-estimated. Money poured in from booty, indemnities, provincial taxes, loans and miscellaneous extractions in quantities without precedent in Graeco-Roman history, and at an accelerating rate. . . Nevertheless, the

116. Ibid., 24.

117. Frank Newport, "Americans Anti-Big Business, Big Gov't," *Gallup*, January 19, 2012.

118. Baumol, "Entrepreneurship."

whole phenomenon is misunderstood when it is classi-
fied under the headings of "corruption" and "malprac-
tice," as historians still persist in doing.[119]

As the final sentence makes clear, these unproductive forms of
entrepreneurship were not—at the time—considered dishonorable.
Corruption was so routine that it was not looked upon as abhorrent
or even unusual. This example may have disturbing implications
if cultural mores encourage entrepreneurs to enter industries that
redistribute rent rather than those that create wealth.

K. Lost Social Trust

Lastly, privilege may entail cultural costs if it weakens the bonds of
social trust. A number of economists have documented the important role that trust plays in fostering growth; when humans are
more likely to trust strangers, they are more likely to do business
with them.[120] Trust, then, facilitates economic exchange. As Senior
World Bank Economist Stephen Knack has put it, "If you take a
broad enough definition of trust, then it would explain basically
all the difference between the per capita income of the United
States and Somalia."[121] Just as trust is a necessary ingredient for
long-run economic growth, a sudden and precipitous collapse in
trust can be the catalyst for a deep and protracted recession.[122]

In his 1999 book *Government's End*, journalist and Brookings
Institution writer in residence Jonathan Rauch extensively documents the link between the rise of special-interest politics and

119. Quoted in Baumol, "Entrepreneurship," 899.

120. Stephen Knack and Philip Keefer, "Does Social Capital Have an Economic
Payoff? A Cross-Country Investigation," *Quarterly Journal of Economics* 112,
no. 4 (November 1997): 1251–1288; Paul Zak and Stephen Knack, "Trust and
Growth," *Economic Journal* 111 (2001): 295–321; and Yann Algan and Pierre Cahuc,
"Inherited Trust and Growth," *American Economic Review* 100, no. 5 (2010):
2060–2092.

121. Quoted in Tim Harford, "The Economics of Trust," Forbes.com, July 2010.

122. Bruce Yandle, "Lost Trust: The Real Cause of the Financial Meltdown" (working paper, Mercatus Center at George Mason University, Arlington, VA, 2009).

the decline of public trust in American democracy.[123] If Rauch's account is accurate and privilege really is correlated with declining trust, economic growth may be threatened. To compound the problem, policy may also get worse because public policy and trust interact in complex ways. Economists Philippe Aghion, Yann Algan, Pierre Cahuc, and Andrei Shleifer recently studied the interaction between government regulation and trust using data from a cross section of countries and from extensive surveys of individuals within those countries.[124] They found that "distrust fuels support for government control over the economy," but "distrust generates demand for regulation even when people realize that the government is corrupt and ineffective; they prefer state control to unbridled production by uncivic entrepreneurs." Most interestingly, they found that trust and regulation "coevolve." Distrust seems to lead to more regulation, but more regulation seems also to lead to more distrust.[125]

IV. CONCLUDING REMARKS

Government-granted privileges are pathological. Privileges limit the prospects for mutually beneficial exchange—the very essence of economic progress. They raise prices, lower quality, and discourage innovation. They pad the pockets of the wealthy and well-connected at the expense of the poor and unknown. When governments dispense privileges, smart, hardworking, and creative people are encouraged to spend their time devising new ways to obtain favors instead of new ways to create value for customers. Privileges depress long-run economic growth and threaten short-run macroeconomic stability. They even undermine cultural

123. Jonathan Rauch, *Government's End: Why Washington Stopped Work* (New York: Public Affairs, 1999); see also John Garen, "How to Spend the Public's Money While Losing the Public's Trust," Special Study, Mercatus Center at George Mason University, forthcoming.

124. Philippe Aghion, Yann Algan, Pierre Cahuc, and Andrew Shleifer, "Regulation and Distrust," *Quarterly Journal of Economics* 125, no. 3 (2010): 1015–1049.

125. Ibid., 1016.

mores, fostering cronyism, blurring the distinction between productive and unproductive entrepreneurship, and eroding people's trust in both business and government.

But for all of the problems with privileges, governments dispense them freely and sometimes proudly. In the 2012 presidential race, for example, both President Obama and former Senator Rick Santorum endorsed lucrative privileges for the manufacturing industry.[126] And at least anecdotal evidence suggests that in the United States, government-granted privileges are becoming more common than ever.

If we are to restore the economy and the body politic to health, we must rout out and eliminate the sources of government-granted privilege. And if our institutions are to remain healthy, we must develop a better understanding of the sources of privilege and the ways to guard against it.

126. President Obama in his 2012 State of the Union address, for example, singled out the manufacturing sector for special tax treatment and support. And in the Republican presidential primary, Rick Santorum has suggested that manufacturing firms—and only manufacturing firms—should be exempted from taxation.

APPENDIX:
Privilege Diminishes the Gains from Exchange

Figure 1, which should be familiar to all students of economics, depicts the mutual gains from trade. The figure shows industry supply and demand curves in a given market. The demand curve, also known as the marginal benefit curve, represents the maximum price that buyers are willing to pay for each quantity purchased. But notice that for every unit sold, the market price that these buyers *actually* pay is less than the amount they would be *willing* to pay (i.e., price is below the industry demand curve). Because they are able to purchase the good for less than what they would be willing to pay for it, these consumers enjoy what economists call "consumer surplus."

Figure 1. The Gains from Free and Voluntary Exchange

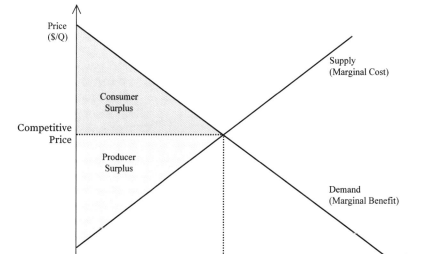

Sellers also gain. The supply curve, also known as the marginal cost curve, represents the minimum price that sellers would be willing to accept for each quantity they sell. Notice that for every unit sold, the market price that these sellers actually receive exceeds the amount that they would be willing to accept (the price is above the industry supply curve). Because they are able to sell the good for more than they would be willing to accept, these producers enjoy what economists call "producer surplus." In a competitive industry, the producer surplus is shared by all producers and represents a "normal return."

As figure 2 shows, a monopolist with pricing power will charge a price that is higher than that charged by a competitive firm.[127] Compared with competitive conditions, consumer surplus is smaller while producer surplus is larger. Since the monopolist is the only firm, it captures the entire producer surplus. Thus, monopoly profits are quite substantial compared with the normal profits of a competitive firm. Note that the sum of producer and consumer surplus under monopoly is less than the sum of producer and consumer surplus under competition. To put it another way, the monopolist gains less than consumers and would-be competitors lose. The lost social gain is known as "deadweight loss" and is indicated in figure 2.

127. The profit maximizing price is that which ensures that the cost of the last unit produced just equals the revenue obtained from that unit. The monopolist's marginal revenue curve traces the revenue received from the last unit sold.

Figure 2. The Costs of Monopoly

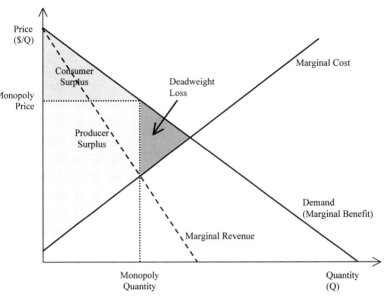

But monopoly privileges may entail more than conventional deadweight loss. Privileged firms are likely to waste resources, leading to higher production costs. Figure 3 depicts this problem with a higher marginal cost curve. This results in so-called "X-inefficiency" costs.[128]

128. Notice that with higher marginal production costs, producer surplus is smaller. This doesn't mean that the firm is necessarily worse off. While its pecuniary benefits are smaller, the managers and workers in the firm enjoy more leisure time at work. Recall Hicks's observation that "the best of all monopoly profits is a quiet life." Hicks, "Annual Survey of Economic Theory."

Figure 3. *X*-Inefficiencies, Inattention to Consumer Desires, and Rent-Seeking

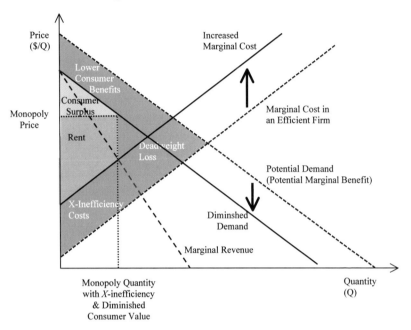

If managers and workers are less attentive to their work, consumers will derive less satisfaction from each product they consume. Thus, the demand curve for a privileged monopolist's product will lie below the potential demand curve. Figure 3 shows this scenario as a downward shift in the demand curve.[129] Because of the diminished demand for its product, the firm will sell less than it otherwise would. Consumers will derive less consumer surplus from exchange and total losses will expand as shown in figure 3.

There are also likely to be rent-seeking losses. The cost of rent-seeking is related to the size of the rent in figure 3. The larger the rent, the more firms will be willing to invest in rent-seeking. But other factors matter as well. For example, rent-seeking losses tend

---

129. This, in turn, means that marginal revenue also lies below its potential. As with higher production costs, it also means that the firm will reap less producer surplus. Here again, Hicks's observation pertains.

to be larger when more firms are competing for the privilege. This scenario is just the opposite of what we expect in a traditional market in which more competition leads to a more efficient outcome.[130] Rent-seeking losses may be larger or smaller than the rent itself.

When all of the costs of privilege are considered, it is possible that only a small fraction of the gains from exchange remain. But even these costs understate the problems with privilege; figure 3 only shows the "static" costs of privilege at a particular point in time. Over time, however, privilege likely entails "dynamic" costs that include lost innovation and slower economic growth.

130. Dennis Mueller, *Public Choice III* (New York: Cambridge University Press, 2003), 335–336.

ABOUT THE AUTHOR

Matthew Mitchell is a senior research fellow at the Mercatus Center at George Mason University. His primary research interests include economic freedom and economic growth, government spending, state and local fiscal policy, public choice, and institutional economics. Dr. Mitchell received his Ph.D. and his M.A. in economics from George Mason University. He received his B.A. in political science and B.S. in economics from Arizona State University. He has testified before the U.S. Congress and his work has been featured in numerous national media outlets, including the *New York Times*, the *Wall Street Journal*, the *Washington Post*, the *Washington Times*, *National Public Radio*, and *C-SPAN*.